#ThereIsMore

By
J.M. Weldon

A Real Talk Media Book

Also by J.M. Weldon

You're Not That Special

The Best [BAD] Advice I've Ever Received

Intertwined
(Published as J. Malik Weldon)

#THEREISMORE

Hashtags and Heartfelt Hopes

By

J.M. Weldon

ISBN: 978-0615969244

REAL TALK MEDIA GROUP
Savannah | Atlanta | DC | New York

For Information:
REAL TALK MEDIA GROUP
P.O. Box 30863
Savannah, Georgia 31410

TheRealTalkNetwork@gmail.com

10   9   8   7   6   5   4   3   2   1

Dedicated to the journey of self-discovery and all those who undertake it.

#Contents

#ThereIsMore

Imagine if you will, the North Pole. This area at geodetic latitude 90° North is not the fabled secret hideout for a fat guy's toy workshop, but rather a vacant spot of the Arctic Ocean littered with floating sea ice. Amidst the floating frozen flotsam here at the highest point of the planet, a voice cries out.

Deep in the plains of the Serengeti, the largest mammal migration on earth is currently underway. The ground is rich with the blood and bones of centuries of fierce warriors, and as the calls of zebras, wildebeests, and buffaloes fill the air, a small voice cries out.

In the bustling metropolis of New York City, where from street to street the scene shifts from high fashion to low income, there is never a moment of silence. But underneath the constant blaring of honking cabs, the cat calls of cavorting teens, and the steady march of a million daily tourists, a faint voice cries out.

Who is calling? What is the message? Can you hear it?

This is the point where an author would generally bore you with an overly used reference to "The Matrix" or a series of facts and figures. However, the truth minus the superfluity is simply this – every person on this planet has a choice to make. The voice that is calling out is the voice of your inner self. It is the confident, the true, the honest, the daring, the real you that you were at birth before this world convinced you to stay in line.

This is NOT a call for you to rebel against society. After all, society is created by mankind for mankind. If you choose to get involved in the political process, either through elected representation or through civil disobedience, you were probably already predisposed to do so before you encountered this book. This is NOT a call for you to become a titan of industry or business. There are far too many books out there giving people the false belief that with four easy steps they can transform their bank accounts from a negative balance to millionaire status, all while collecting unemployment insurance and living in their mother's basement. That is not real, and this book is all about the real. This is a book by a real guy who deals with real life situations every day, just like you. We all triumph and we fail. And we do these both exceptionally and irrelevantly. This is NOT a call to conquer the world. If I knew how to do so, I would probably do so myself, if not for the worry that the stress would cause me bleeding ulcers. After all, who wants to rule 7 billion people? I have trouble getting my kids to listen to me for longer for 5 minutes without getting distracted. And if you are like me, which I presuppose you are, you are not looking to control the world more than you are truly looking for some control over *your* world.

That is what this is. This is a call to a realization. A simple truth that echoes throughout every fiber of your being. You are a sleeping giant. And the voice within you is struggling to emit a suppressed scream. We have searched from the mountain's peaks to the ocean's depth to the furthest reaches of space to answer one essential question: "Who am I?" And all the while, we have known. The earth has known. Our very DNA has known. The blood coursing through our veins has known. We are alive. And the voice that cries out is the voice within us. The eternal internal call for us to recognize that every time we accept a false reality we fall deeper into the trance that keeps us from the real us. The simple continuous call that cries out: "WAKE UP."

What are the things that keep us locked in this hypnotic state, sleepwalking our way through our very existence? We say that our responsibilities, our financial shortcomings, our upbringing, even our race or socioeconomic status prevent us from becoming all the things we want. However, the mere fact that you desire more than you have is evidence that you are aware that you have heard the call to wake up. Those truly asleep accept the current state of their lives as reality and, acquiescing to the belief that nothing will ever change, submit to being molded by their experiences rather than molding their lives like the titans they are inside.

There are those who hear the call to wake up, but choose to ignore or delay their rise to reality. This is usually due to one of the false beliefs listed above. I call this the "Snooze

Excuse." Much like hitting the snooze button on an alarm clock, this postponement of the advent of the day does not prevent the world from turning; it simply excuses you from joining in while creating an excuse of why you can't possibly rise at this given moment. And because the world around you is more than happy to keep you subdued in slumber, your sense of self-justification of all the things you can't do is easily accepted.

Then there is the reverse of the "I can't do anything" crowd. There is the unrealistic "I can do and have it all – right now" belief. But that's a good thing right? They have awoken and claimed their place in the world. They are kings, they are leaders, they are... mistaken. There is nothing wrong with wanting it all. There is nothing wrong with having it all. It is the "right now" part that becomes worrisome. The misconception that the universe or the government or even God will hand you a million dollars, a beach house, a Fortune 500 company, and a swimsuit model just because you want it is ridiculous. Everything in this world is obtainable, by working for it. I do not discount the often true statement of "it's not what you know, it's who you know," but unless the person you know is a close relative with millions in disposable income, you are going to have to work for yours. However, nowadays there is a purveying principle that if you want something enough, it will be drawn to you simply by virtue of your desire. I'm all for faith, but blind faith in magical theories is quite simply hogwash. But yet it is what the sleeping society wants. They have heard the call within, but out of fear or laziness they use the latest fad to continue to hit the snooze button on their existence. As a consequence books, tapes, and seminars on the pseudo-scientific law of attraction and power of thought continue to sell out. This belief has proven so lucrative that it has even infiltrated contemporary religion, where preachers eager to grow congregations and bank accounts have instituted a message of "if you want it, it's yours," often encouraging followers to make a financial donation as evidence of their faith in receiving material possessions. Not only is the message contrary to the entire message of these religions, many of which were founded on the concepts of caring for the poor and widows while storing treasures in Heaven based on righteous living on Earth, but it also shows the need to heed the voice within us frantically trying to stop the deception we accept and get us to WAKE UP.

Anything worth having is worth working for. That is a simple truth that has existed as long as man. I am not against working smarter instead of harder, but there are no magic lamps with wish-granting genies that will get us through life. But that has not been the mindset or experience for many in today's culture.

For some of us, our parents were those genies, never allowing us to have to endure the tough but lesson-learning experience that comes with falling off a bike or dealing with a bad grade on a science exam. They jumped in to keep us safe, and then the safety led to coddling, and the coddling led to spoiling. Then one of two things happened, they either threw us out in the world completely unprepared or they continue to rescue us well into adulthood. Either way, it is next to impossible to reach your potential when you are never allowed to fail, to fall, and then ultimately grow from the experience.

For others of us, there is such a disengagement from reality that if we can't have the world handed to us on a silver platter then we just choose not to participate. I have encountered many people that refuse to finish school or work a full-time job because they have to make it their way or no way at all. These people are musicians waiting on a big break, but crashing on a friend's couch in the meantime. They are athletes that are so confident in their jump shot that they won't bother to crack open a history book. These are the laid off worker, so dismayed by the harsh sting of rejection, collecting unemployment or worker's compensation and spending it on lottery tickets. These people are deluding themselves; they say they are waiting on that one big moment to change everything, when in actuality they are pressing the snooze excuse to block out any world in which their dream doesn't happen as they imagine it. Let's assume their dreams come true. What if that 25-year-old musician gets his big break to top charts... at age 40? How will he live in the meantime? What if that athlete gets drafted to the NBA and breaks his ankle in his first game? What will he fall back on? What will that out-of-work man do when he wins the lottery and has no concept of financial management? Will he be right back where he started a year later?

The point of this is simply that dreams are wonderful, but not wonderfully practical.

However, peppered with the knowledge that really big dreams require a really big commitment, you can accomplish anything in this life. But you have to WAKE UP. Not many of us have a rich uncle bequeathing us a fortune nor are we so talented that we can walk into any profession and excel. For the majority of us, we get out of life what we put into it. And in order to take that first step, we have to get out of bed. It's time to stop living our lives like we are in a movie, and start living a life that will inspire a movie. But what gives me the right to speak on or down to these visionaries? Because they are me and I am them.

#TheRealMe

While I will never claim to be a world class athlete, I was what I thought to be a great writer. As a child music was not entertainment to me; it was a living entity flowing in the air all around me. It was a language I understood that others did not, and at times it was my only friend. My favorite thing to do was create melodies and songs out of every day events and conversations. Before I had graduated high school, I had a notebook of over 150 original songs I had written. To date, I have written, arranged, produced or composed over 300 songs in various genres and released three independent albums.

Back in middle school, my love of reading exploded with a free period and an expansive school library. I poured through the juvenile mysteries like my peers, and then moved on to classics. I would grab the books my older siblings were required to read for their high school classes and devour their secrets. Then my love for fiction was solidified at age 12 when I read "Lightning" by Dean R. Koontz on a school trip for Quiz Bowl. It was vivid writing like I had never before experienced. I was captivated and quickly became a Koontz fan, spending my allowance to build a library of his books (before I realized I could check them out at my local library). Every work was distinctive; some were suspense, some science fiction, some mysterious love stories, and others flat out horror, but they all had that same writing signature. And I discovered something: when I read good writing, I created good writing. I soon began regaling my classmates with short stories of imagined exploits involving alien abductions, break-ins to the secret vault that held items confiscated in class, shoot-outs with our hated social studies teacher, and even trips to brothels (I was a very creative kid).

My stories brought me attention I previously had unable to obtain, and I loved it. It was the opinion of my peers that I would inevitably become a world famous author, and I naturally agreed. So at the age of thirteen I decided that my path was clear: write the great American novel, become rich and famous, win a Pulitzer, and retire by age 30 and live off book sales. It didn't quite happen that way. For years I attempted to write that novel. I got about ten pages in on most tries. The next attempt, the story was completely different. Why was I unable to complete my chosen – nay, destined – path? Well for one, after I concluded that was my life path, I just sat back and waited for it to happen. I never took the time to learn all the things I needed to learn to become a rich and famous author. As a matter of fact, at age thirteen I stopped learning altogether. Sure I went to school, I graduated, even attended college, but I never worked a day after my revelation. I assumed I knew my life and just had to wait for it to come to me (my own unrecognized law of attraction). High school was a breeze with the exception for science and math, which I got through by memorization and a homeroom class committed to copying each other's homework. As for me, I wrote papers, took tests, and passed as I was expected to. It was not until my freshman year of college at Emory University that I realized I had no idea how to study because I had never done it. I was simply a good listener and could verbally regurgitate information. However, in college you have independent learning, thought, and you are paying for the right to grow. It was not in line with my mindset. I was going to be a Pulitzer winning novelist and the only deviation from the plan was the addition of me becoming a Grammy award winning songwriter.

Plenty of people tried to help me. I had counselors and professors at every turn warning me that without the work I would fail. They offered tutoring, they offered extra credit;

they offered the world to me, as long as I would try. I refused (or more likely agreed and then never showed up). Instead I distracted myself with video games, girls, and alcohol. And I flunked out. I returned home in disgrace and enrolled in a state school. Once again I had the big fish in a small pond feeling I had throughout my high school career. Once again, I let the belief drive my actions... or rather inactions. This time, I was sure to succeed. I joined the music program to expand my repertoire while retaking the simple classes I had failed at my previous college. I did really good...for a year. I had caught up to where I should have been, and was time to do the real work. Now an English major and Music minor, I had advisors promoting various career paths from being a teacher to an editor to greeting card or jingle writer. All I heard, though, was NOT world famous novelist / songwriter. In my own mind I was the embodiment of a modern day Ernest Hemingway and Cole Porter, though I had produced absolutely nothing to make anyone else regard me as such.

Around this time, I began to find ways to distract myself from the looming reality of the irrationality of my dreams. I pledged a fraternity, started a series of fun albeit destructive relationships, and participated in a number of theater productions (which added Tony award winning actor to my "give-me" life list) while writing my first musical play. I kept my grades up, but began attending class less and less, which led to several grades of Incomplete at this school where attendance mattered just as much as test responses. Finally I was asked to sit out a semester and reevaluate my commitment to my education. I was so offended by what I perceived as a second-rate school suspending me that I just moved away and never went back.

More than ten years later here I am. Five years of college. Three different universities.

Zero degrees. No Pulitzer or Grammy or Tony Award. This doesn't mean it cannot still happen for me. It means simply one thing that it took me many years of menial jobs in which I was constantly asked "why are you working *here*?" to realize. Anything worth having is worth working for. Nothing is handed to you. The reward in creating something good is the creation itself. Not the accolades you desire because you feel a need for validation. The price is the work it took you to get there, and the prize is getting there. My life plan has taken twists and turns. I've spent time as a salesman, a banquet server, a minister, a freelance business writer, a poet, a security guard, an internet marketing pro, loan officer and more. But those are just things I have done. We've all worn many hats, filled many roles, worked at many jobs, but is that all there is to us? I say no. I am more than what I've done, and I am more than what I've been through. True, I am an ex-husband, a father to two great kids, a son who was thrown to the world unprepared but eventually found his way, an eternal student once again attempting to fix the mistakes of the past. But I am also whatever I choose to work towards being. I am what I put my focus and energy towards. I am more than my past or my wants. I am more, and so are you

One day, I lost everything. And in doing so, I gained the world. I'll spare you the long, sad tale of my demise, not because I think it will bore you, but rather because I'm done living in it. Here's the thing, though, when the life that I had built (or rather fell into from inaction) came apart at the seams, I had a unique opportunity to build myself anew. That is when my search for purpose truly began. No longer was I operating based on what others said they saw in me. No longer was I merely reacting to the circumstances around me. I was, for once, creating my own reality. And the more I started to ask myself "Who am I?"

the more I found the answers in the stripping away of what I wasn't.

I began to see there was so much that I just accepted about life that made no sense. The political structure was corrupt, yet I celebrated my favored candidate and vilified any and all opposition. There was such compassionless apathy towards the less fortunate that I found myself participating in, knowing full well that wasn't how I really felt. When I felt hurt I hid my pain in order to be seen as masculine; when I felt proud I contained my enthusiasm so as to not seem arrogant. I noticed more and more that there were so many masks that we all wore every day just to ride the tide of public opinion. And more and more, the fallacy of my life began to sicken me. So I did the only thing I really know how to do: I wrote.

At first it started as a blog about my personal journey. I felt as if I had lost something; the passion that had once propelled me forward had disappeared. I tried to think back on my life to determine where I went off track. I pondered old relationships, my employment history, the economy, my struggles with weight loss. But it never really got to the heart of the issue because, as I discovered, the past is just that – the past. You can learn from it, but dwelling in it and on it only serve to keep it alive. I had to look at the bigger picture. I saw all around people sleepwalking through their lives, much as I had. Then as I migrated my thoughts onto Facebook, I posed the question: "Why is the world the way it is?"

I started to talk about some of my personal shortcomings and my efforts to forgive myself and move on. I wrote about how the feeling of separation was so soul crushing, and how real and visceral love can be. I expounded on my fears of not being significant and delved into my confusion of the value system of our society. And to my surprise, my words resonated with others.

There came a shift in me as I noticed that I was not alone in this search. I understood that somehow we had as a species had gotten off course. We had become so technologically advanced, and yet had become so spiritually bankrupt. We saw each other as opponents instead of allies. We saw nature as an obstacle to trample instead of a rich tapestry of life. I had no choice but to change my thinking. That's not to say I am the epitomic transcended man; no, far from it. What it means is I came to realize there is so much that actually mattered that I was ignoring in order to concentrate on irrelevant distractions. I had been thinking of the Law of Attraction as a magic genie to bring me things, but I saw now that the magic was in me. By thinking on negative things, I was making myself into a negative person. So by focusing on the beauty in the world, I could create a beautiful existence. It's not about physical things, it's about my mind and soul and overall wellbeing. Because life is not just about material possessions, life is so much more. Life is about connections and emotions and experiences and developing yourself and listening to your heart and following your intuition and helping others and freedom and forgiveness and passion and purpose and transcending the status quo and so much more. That's the point. Everything we have been settling for is not enough. There is more... and it's inside you... waiting to be revealed.

The following pages contain my thoughts, my dreams, my hopes, both for myself and for you. Many of these are direct quotes from posts from my various social media accounts. Most have been edited for this project.

I am not your guru. I am your friend. I am your brother. I write these words to you because you matter to me. Because separation is a lie. Because we are all one. Because there is more.

#THEREISHOPE

#ThereIsMore

There is a hidden treasure within you. Some believe that you have to seek your destiny, but I think you should first seek yourself. Become who you want to be, and allow your new nature to fortify you in your lack and bring you wisdom in your surplus.

This is not the Law of Attraction, where thinking about things brings you in contact with them. This is inward reflection, where you take stock of your faults and forgive yourself and make a change for the better... every day. This is empathy, where you become sensitive to other people's struggle and seek to alleviate their pain. This is Love, the most powerful force on the planet, for when you become one with it, it is reflected all around you and returned to you 100-fold. This is hope, this is faith, and most importantly, this is possible.

#YouAreMore

Okay, let's get serious for a minute. I want to talk to you… about you. Because if you're anything like me, you're settling. Every day in a million different ways we talk ourselves out of being our authentic, awesome self. And it's our mind's fault; it's been condition to keep us at a safe, manageable level.

We see a homeless man with a sign asking for help and self says no one should live like that, but mind tells us to mind our business and keep moving.

We sit at a red light and notice an amazing sunset and self says take in the glory of this world, but mind says stay in your lane and go before people start honking.

We have dreams of travel and self says take six months off and see the world, but mind says that's not practical, just work all year and save for a week vacation to the same resort you visited last year.

There is a voice inside of us, begging us to elevate our self past our mind. You can be more: more motivated, more determined, more present, more intuitive, more adventurous, more compassionate, more creative, more alive. More of the you that you desire to be in the moment before your mind talks you out of it.

I believe in this, not just as an outside observer but as someone who knows I've not been living up to my potential. It's not an overnight transition, but it is an immediate decision, and I'm thankful for the opportunity to take the first of a million steps into the more I was always meant to be.

Won't you join me? Won't you please just believe... in you?

#TrustAgain

I was reminded of something today. We often close the door to future possibilities because of our past experiences. In fact, we even call it experience, as in "In my experience, men are all dogs" or "In my experience, people cannot be trusted."

The thing that we have to realize is that at one time you took a chance in order to have that prior experience. So why would you refuse to take such chances again? When you get hungry and eat, later don't you get hungry again... and eat again? But your experience tells you that the food didn't permanently satisfy your hunger, so why try it again? And if you have a sandwich and it was good, then why go against your experience and have soup or salad or pizza next time?

It is because a part of you knows, even subconsciously, that one encounter (whether positive or negative) doesn't define you.

What I'm trying to say, in my own roundabout way, is that experience is good, but experiences are what make a life. Don't be so ruled by your past that you ruin any chance at a future.

Fear is a lie.

Try again.

Trust again.

Love again.

Live again.

#DivineConnections

There are some people that, due to having years of personal history with, you'd do anything for. They have shown themselves to be a positive influence in your life, and despite how much time passes between communic-ation, they will always be a part of you.

Then there are those rare occasions when you meet someone and instantly feel that connection. Sometimes it's romantic, other times simply platonic, but there is a tangible bond between you. It's almost as if the frequencies of your souls come together, intertwining and co-mingling, creating a kinship on par with family or lover.

If you are graced to find this connection, and it is reciprocated, please embrace it! Don't let your "common sense" (which is mostly merely societal conditioning) rob you of a divine relationship.

Recognize that yes, sometimes you are drawn to people because of shared insecurities or strengths, and little else exists under the surface. But other times you are being compelled towards a something much greater, and that chance alone is worth the experience.

After all, isn't one of the best things in the world just finding another person who gets you?

#YouMadeIt

Congratulations! There are a lot of people that didn't make it to this day. Some were taken unfairly. Some spent long lives and went peacefully into the night. Some were overtaken by sadness and gave up the precious gift of life. But you my friend, you are still here. You still have a chance to chase your dreams, to love and be loved, and to create the strongest version of yourself. You have endless possibilities before you. That's what life is: not the drudgery of employment, not even the joy of family. Life is possibility. And every day that you live on anything could happen. And if that's not a reason to smile, I don't know what it is.

#Belief

Belief is a funny thing. Some of us subscribe to the idea of an intelligent designer, a grand creator, and others do not. But we all have faith. When we sit down on a chair we believe that it will hold our weight. When we walk into our home we believe that the roof won't collapse on our heads. We go to sleep at night believing we will wake in the morning. We turn the key or press the start button in our cars believing they will start. We all have faith in something. Why then, would we not have faith in another person? Why not believe in the power of love? Why not have faith in the greatness that could be? And moreover, why not believe in you? In your worth? In your dreams? In your ability to make it right this time? Why not just believe?

I'm not telling you what I think. I'm telling you what I live. I'm telling you what I believe.

#Hopeful

Someone out there has been waiting for what you have to offer. The question is: "Will you be too busy hiding what's in you for them to find it?"

Life is hard. And messy. And it's far easier to dwell on what didn't work than to hope for a better, brighter day. But sometimes hope is all you have left... after your best laid plans get derailed. It's your choice to be hopeless or Hope-Full.

#Simple

Ask yourself the question,
"What do I truly desire?"

Then tell yourself,
"It's time to go get it."

Maybe life really is that simple.

Maybe we make things more difficult than
they need to be.

Maybe today is the day we simplify...
and finally get all we've been waiting for.

#TakeYouBack

People take from you all day. They take your time. They take your energy. They take your patience. They take your money. They take your hope. Here's something you can take... take a chance. Like someone? Tell them. Want a job? Apply. Want to know something? Ask. Because in the end you'll probably regret the things you were too afraid to try more than the adventures you were bold enough to take. Take "you" back.

#TGIN

Welcome to today. The only day you know you have. Whether or not it is a good day is completely up to you, because concepts like good and bad are subjective terms. My thinking is, though, if you woke up, feel reasonably well, have the freedom to go and do as you please, and possess the power to give and receive love, then there is far more to celebrate than to complain about. So smile my friends, at long last we made it. Today is finally here, and this could be a day to remember, the day our lives change forever... for the better.

Thank God It's Now.

#BeHappy

There is this moment every morning, as I'm preparing to face the world, that I have to figure out who I am, what I'm doing, where I'm going, and how I'll be. I place on the forced mask of professional, studious, active, patient, industrious, etc. whether or not I'm feeling that way, because that is what the day requires of me. However this day has no expectations, no to do list, no overwhelming responsibilities. This day is mine to do as I please. And after careful consideration I have made the following determination: I think I will be happy today.

You're more than welcome to join me.

#BelieveAgain

Remember when you believed in magic?
Remember when you believed in fairy tales?
Remember when you believed in endless
possibilities? Remember when you believed in
the goodness in us all? Remember when you
believed in a life of greater meaning?

Remember when you believed... in yourself?

Believe again.
And I'll believe with you.

#Bedtime

As you lay in your bed this evening, wrapped in the comfort of the night, listening to the lullaby of your steady breath tuned to the metronome of your heartbeat, and the cares of the day begin to melt off of you, and you return to the essence of you, make a mental note of that presence of peace and harmony overtaking you. And when the morning's light wakes you to see another day, arise and live out that love like the person you really are.

#KeepGoing

Life is tough. You are tougher.
You know that weight on your shoulders?
That one you thought was crushing you?
It's actually making you stronger with every
step you take.

Keep going.

#Enough

You.
Are.
Enough.

#*Glorious*

Can I share something with you?
It's kind of a secret, so come close.
Jeez, this is a little embarrassing but I need to
be honest about something.

I think you are absolutely amazing. Really. I
know it hasn't always been easy for you, but,
wow, you are still here. I am so proud of you.
Seriously. Do you know what you are capable
of? I mean, you must have an inkling of it
because it radiates off of you. But I need you to
know that despite the fact that you might not
be where you want to be, you are exactly who
you need to be. You are glorious. You are
powerful. You are enough. I believe in you.

#SeeYourself

If you could see yourself through my eyes, you'd never doubt yourself again. I believe in you. Even when you don't. I see the more that is in you. And trust me when I tell you, it's beautiful.

#LoveGlasses

If only they made glasses for the heart, then we might be able to see each other more clearly.

If only we knew the struggles that others endure, then we might be more careful with our words.

If only we listened to the things people don't say out loud, then we might understand that we are not that different after all.

#Perception

I bought a new mirror today. The price was reduced 40%. The cashier said it had been returned because the person who bought it said her reflection looked horrible in it, and since she was clearly very attractive, the mirror had to be warped. "That's strange," I said as I handed him my money, "When I look in it all I see is awesome." He laughed, and said "Well maybe it's not the mirror; maybe she should get her eyes checked." I responded as I gathered my package, "Maybe that's just the way she sees herself; perhaps she should get her heart checked." It's all about perception.

#BeYourself

Sometimes I think I can get away with certain things because of my innate charm, machismo, million dollar smile, and red hot animal magnetism. Then I remember I don't have any of those things. But what I am, however, is original and awkward and awesome. And that seems to be working out just fine so far.

#MoveOn

I get it. You've been hurt. People have done you wrong. You made some stupid mistakes. Okay, a lot of them. But here's the thing. The past is gone. You can't change it, and living in it will cause you to miss out on the possibilities that are all around you at this very moment. It's been said that opportunity is not a lengthy visitor, and good fortune (like bad) comes when you least expect it. But that is life: a beautiful, crazy, haphazard, messy, glorious experience. Not everyone is out to get you. Not every relationship ends with a broken heart. And you are not destined to repeat the past... unless you keep yourself in it. It's time to move on. Give life a chance. Give yourself a chance.

#KeepGoing

Keep going. Shed the weight of yesterday. Smile at the possibilities of tomorrow. Live in the beauty of today.

#OneThing

Out of all the various ideas, concepts, theologies, theories, opinions, lifestyles and traditions in the world, if you only choose one thing to believe in, I sincerely hope you choose yourself.

#YouMatter

You matter. You could look back over your life and see it as a series of mistakes, hardships, disappointments. You could regret the chances you took that went wrong and regret the chances you never had the courage to take. Or you could see your life as an epic story, continually writing itself through every success and failure, weaving a tale so elaborate that when it reaches the right reader, everything will finally make sense. Someone is waiting for what you have to offer. And in the meantime, why not simply enjoy the ride?

#Experience

You see, the thing people fail to realize is that the low points of our lives are as remarkably breathtaking as the highs. When you begin to step outside of the feeling caused by the experience then you understand the whole point of the experience was to get you to feel. Instead of complaining, instead of avoiding, stop, breathe, be, and feel. That is life, and it's happening all around you.

#*Vision*

I love how when you open yourself up to something, it flows to you. This is true of vision, healing, forgiveness, even love. The first step of getting what you want is breaking free of the lie that you don't deserve it. You are already all that you need. And that means you either have the knowledge, resources, and determination to get it, or you have the capability to endure whatever life throws your way on the journey to getting it. Listen to your heart, and hear where it's leading you. I know you can. And if a nobody like me wholeheartedly believes in you, then you'd be crazy not to believe in yourself. Let's get it!

#Selah

Faith. It's what we choose.
Hope. It's what we have.
Love. It's what we are.

Selah.

#YouMatter

You matter.
That is all.

#FollowYourHeart

Sometimes, in the midst of sound advice, good judgment, and clear logic, the right answer is the one you feel most deeply. That's when you have to ignore what you've been taught and go with what you know.

FOLLOW YOUR HEART.

#BePresent

It's funny how you can speak a thousand words of encouragement and never come close to the emotion and significance of simply being there for someone. More than what you know, more than what you say, what you do truly makes a difference. Be present. It shows people that they are important to you. And everyone wants to feel they matter.

#AllThereIs

Dreams are meant to be dreamt.
Time is meant to be spent.
Life is meant to be lived.
Now is all we get.

She is hers and he is his.
Love is ours to get and give.
Win or lose -- at least you did.
Now is all there is.

The soul cries out to let it lead.
With every deed our heart is freed.
The greatest tree was once a seed.
Now is all we need.

You and I are each unique.
Bold and strong or meek and weak.
Clawing, scraping to reach our peak.
Now is all we seek.

Moments you can feel.

Destiny fulfilled.
The only eternal deal.
Now is all that's real.

#KeepClimbing

They say faith moves mountains. I say faith moves me up the mountain. It's not always the destination that determines, sometimes it's the climb that takes you from who you are to who you can be.

Keep climbing.

#ImWithYou

What do I want from you? Nothing. What do I want for you? Everything. My desire is that you realize the unlimited potential inside of you, the unsurpassed beauty you possess, the unyielding power of your spirit, and that you experience the unveiling of an unimaginably extraordinary life. If I can help you on your journey, without sacrificing my own, I gladly will. For you see, a big part of my dream is to bear witness to the fulfillment of yours.

#THEREIsCHANGE

#TheMessage

There's a thought that keeps reverberating through my mind. A simple message that echoes in my thoughts and emotions. One word that continually alerts me to stop waiting for the perfect moment... to believe in my abilities... to trust in what I've always known... to move into my destiny. That word is "NOW."

Maybe this is a message for all of us. Maybe the shift that has been taken place, the awakening that is sweeping the globe, maybe it was all leading up to this moment. I can't decide for you. But I can stand beside you. Who knows how much time we have left. Wouldn't you rather spend your days pursuing your passions than regretting not taking a chance? I'm just a messenger. The rest is up to you. But I believe.

#TheShift

Live and Love like there's no tomorrow. This pretty much sums up my outlook on life. We've all experienced enough hate, pain, heartache, envy, and misery. We've put our lives on hold trying to fit where we were never meant to. Instead of waiting for the rest of humanity to change, let us begin the work within us. The future will be a brighter place if we shine our light now. Let's get out there and LIVE AND LOVE. There's no time like the present.

#ThePower

We have the power to create the world we desire. One mind, one heart, one life at a time. It all begins in you. Let love rule.

#YouMadeIt

Let's be honest, you did not get to this point in your life alone. There were people (friends, relatives, teachers, employers, angels, strangers) that helped you further your goals and inspired you to keep pushing. And while it's nice and even proper to recognize and thank these people for their assistance, it is vital that you understand that the reason that you made it to today is because of YOU. Even with every privilege, handout, and boost, you had to make a conscious decision to not give up, to not die, to drag yourself out of bed and face one more day. If I could encourage you to remember one thing it is to acknowledge and appreciate yourself. Self-love is a dying art in this overly humble and increasingly interconnected world. Everyone matters, yes it's true, but remember that everyone also includes you.

#Community

One of the most magical yet unintended outcomes of social media is that we create a community of trust. I share myself with you, you share yourself with me. We are trusting each other with our thoughts, dreams, hopes, life events, sense of humor, artwork, music preferences, family information, pictures, even our negativity and grievances (which we usually try to hide from those we meet in the physical world). That's big!

Imagine going up to a stranger on the street and saying "Hello, I'd like to tell you how I feel about my job and show you a photo of my cousin's new baby. Oh, and would you like to play a game with me?" That would never happen, but this is what we do online every single day, with every single post.

We are becoming a more open and embracing people, more likely to build relationships based on communication and honesty, because we feel safer sharing our souls and living our truth. It is truly a gift to find others who accept and evolve you into a more open and trusting individual. The greatest connections are the ones you can trust with the real you, in all of its madness, misery, and magnificence.

#PayItForward

A little while back, I went to the doctor for a
physical and struck up a conversation with the
nurse there. She was having me sign some
paperwork and handed me her pen, but then
said "Make sure I get that pen back." I noted
that it was a nice pen, signed the papers and
gave it back. While she was drawing my blood
she told me that she was used to have a whole
bunch of those nice pens at home but since she
brought them to work they kept going missing.
That one was her last remaining pen. She went
on to tell me that her boyfriend was the one
that bought the pens, but was deployed in the
Army, and she wasn't sure where he got them.
Her story stuck with me, and so I did a little
research online and found a store that sold
those pens. A week later, when I was heading
back to the doctor's office to get my results, I
purchased a pack of the pens and an adhesive
gift bow. I arrived and saw her, still with that
pen, though she told me that she had since lost

the cap. I met with the doctor, and as I was leaving, I placed the box of pens (and bow) on the counter in the exam room. On my way out the door, I went to the counter and said "I think you left something in that room." She got up to check, and I walked out the door.

I'm not telling this story to make myself look good. I've done more messed up stuff in my life than I care to admit. I'm nobody's hero. But I realize there is a real life-changing power in actively listening to others, and showing empathy.

A lot of us spend our lives waiting for a miracle to fall out of the sky and never realize the miracle we have inside of us for someone else. It cost me ten bucks and ten minutes to show someone that they matter. How would it inspire you if you were the recipient of a not-so-random act of kindness? Imagine what would happen if we all just cared enough to care.

#Anticipation

One of the things that excites me most about this life is that there are these undiscovered parts of us all that are bubbling right before the surface, causing an intense anticipation, preparing to explode all over our preconceived notions and reveal not only the beauty of this world but the majesty of our souls. We feel it coming, but we really have no idea just how ridiculously glorious we are. Oh, but we will... and I can't wait. There is so much more to you than you give yourself credit for. Don't believe me, just watch.

#Stagnancy

If all you do is stay in the same place doing the same things in the same way with the same people, you're not moving. You may call it a routine; it could just as easily be called a rut. If 5, 10, 20 years pass by and your life hasn't had any major changes, that's called stagnancy. And stagnancy to the human soul is on par with death. Revive your life! I'm not saying pack up and move to Bora Bora (unless that's your thing), but you can do something. Get a new hairstyle, join a book club, learn an instrument, remodel your home, find a cause you believe in and dedicate yourself to it, go back to school, switch careers, make some new friends (even on the internet), travel a little.

The point is change is good. The timeline of our lives are meant to have more significant points on it than just birth and death. Change is good... and the greatest changes are those that occur within us.

#TalkLessThinkMore

As someone who is overly aware and
perceptive of moods, energies, and sounds, I've
come to realize that many people just talk for
the sake of talking, and have no real purpose
behind their words.

Sometimes it's because they don't have the
courage to confront the person they need to
speak with, like the co-worker that complains
to you about a lazy team member but never
says anything to that person. Or the husband
and wife that vent about the other's annoying
habits to friends, but love each other too much
to ask their partner to change, though both
gladly would.

Sometimes people just talk because they want
to be heard, be recognized, feel significant,
even if what ends up coming out of their
mouth is at best misdirected and at worse
damaging to all involved.

It's the same with our posts online, unresolved issues come blasting through our status updates, causing casual acquaintances to accuse us of dramatics and true friends to either adopt our frustrations or wish we'd get it together. And I say we because I'm guilty of this too. I've had my share of passive aggressive conversations and sarcastic asides. But as the saying goes, the things that we dislike in others reveal more about what we need to change in ourselves.

So I was thinking, maybe we could all work on saying what we need to say to the people we need to say it to, stopping the offense in its tracks, and taking a moment before we speak to think how hearing what we are about to say would make us feel. Sometimes the best conversations are the ones without words.

#Somebody

You know that person you've been trying to please, the one named Everybody? Well I have some news for you, you will never please Everybody. So instead of letting Everybody make you feel like Nobody, why don't you realize that you are indeed Somebody, and start by doing right by you. Just a thought.

#ChangeTheWorld

If they can change the world for the worse, why can't we change it for the better? Your voice matters. We are the difference makers.

#BeTheChange

When you get fed up. When you get discouraged. When you look around at the problems of the day and wonder why somebody doesn't do something. When you find yourself waiting for a sign, a moment, a hero. Remember this: we are the ones we've been waiting for. If you want to see the world change, start with yourself.

#Inside

Questions constantly swirl through your mind. Guess what? You already have the answer in your heart.

Trust Yourself.

#BeAwesome

This is what I'm thinking: being prepared for the worst is well and good, but stressing and constantly thinking about doom and gloom serves no one. Why not change your mindset, from one of expecting misery to anticipating greatness? Why not hop out your bed with a smile on your face and some pep in your step and go forth into this world and be awesome? What if that joy in you spreads to another... and another... and another; until the ones causing the strife become the ones beseeching you for the secret to your contentment?

Something's coming. And this time it's something good. I can feel it. Can you?

#AdventureTime

Wake up...
Literally
Figuratively
Metaphorically
Physically
Emotionally
Mentally
Spiritually
Politically
To the truth
To your potential
To the beauty all around you
And live your dreams
And try again
And believe.

Choose your own adventure.

#TrustButVerify

We live in a culture of information overload and short attention spans. The end result is people form snap judgments based on sensationalist headlines without bothering to delve into a story's content or credibility. Such are the days of the Information Age, where mainstream news organizations cater to corporate interests and every nutcase with a webpage thinks he's a journalist.

That's why now more than ever, one needs to develop discernment and hone intuition. For when credible sources become incredulous, you can always rely on your inner source to determine your personal truth.

#TheDeception

We've been lied to. By our governments, by our teachers, by the media, by various religions, often by our friends and families, by both viciously corrupt and well-meaning individuals. Sometimes it's an intentional obfuscation; sometimes it's just the propagation of long accepted beliefs. We've even lied to ourselves. It's evident every time we see the world as us vs. them. For the real deception is separation. And the truth is we are all one.

#Acceptance

I am different than you, but I am not better
than you... and vice-versa. If I buy into the idea
that I am superior, then along the way I might
believe I have the right to rule or abuse or own
or destroy you... and vice-versa. And this is the
fallacy that causes a grieving world to weep.
And I may just be one man, but I believe that
we are better suited dropping love bombs than
atomic ones.

#DontQuit

I know things seem bleak at times. The world
is falling apart. You want to make a difference,
but you can barely pay your rent or mortgage
on time. You have dreams that mean the world
to you, and they might as well be on another
world for how far away they seem. It's easier to
acquiesce to the mindless distractions than to
risk disappointment pursuing important goals.
But there is one thing that no economy, no war,
no person can take from you... and that is your
hope. Only you can give that up. So I have a
message for you on the edge about to throw in
the towel. DON'T.

#LifeEqualsChange

A lot of people are hesitant to take steps towards change because they don't want be labeled hypocrites based on their past declarations. What they fail to realize is that everyone makes claims and decisions based on the information they have access to at the time. The world is in a state of constant flux, and you should be learning and growing during each part of your journey. Holding tight to the traditions and mindset of the past, not because you believe in them but because you are afraid of looking foolish in the eyes of others, is the same as being a functioning adult still wearing diapers because no one else around bothered to get potty trained. Be foolish. Stand out. Follow your own path. And if the road you travel turns out to be a lonely one, at least it will be one that is true.

#RandomActsOfKindness

When was the last time you did something nice
for no reason at all... except that it was nice? A
kind word to friend you haven't spoken to in a
while; seeing the "How Am I Driving" sign on
a truck and then calling to say the driver's
doing a good job; sincerely thanking a busy
cashier for helping you; hearing that a friend is
moving and offering to help them before they
even ask; complimenting a co-worker on their
job performance. These things don't cost you
anything but your time, and the happiness you
give will more than make up for that. Want
love? Start by giving love. Soon you will
become love. You'll never know what pain
your smile can heal.

#MadeForMore

Go to school. Get good grades. Go to a good college so you can get a good job. Work diligently so you can buy a house you can't afford and never spend any time in because you are always at the office trying to earn money to pay for it. Get married young and have 2.5 kids and leave them to fend for themselves while you work yourself into an early grave doing something that you hate to provide for the people that you love. Spend 30 years on your job and retire -- no, spend 8 years and get laid off, then spend 3 years getting back on your feet, then spend 4 years underemployed while back in school learning new skills, then spend 20 years on a new job (five of which you're working a second job to help with the kids' college tuition). Plan your retirement for 60, but not be able to afford the cost of living so keep working until you're 67 and no company can find any further use for you. Spend your life thinking of all the wonderful places you'll travel to once you can afford it, and then wake up one day and realize that your health is too poor and your debt is too high and the world is too dangerous for you to explore. And sit back and look around and all the stuff in your life and realize you would happily trade it all in for more time with the ones you love.

Now wake up. Realize that wherever you are right now, no matter your situation, it is not too late. You can adjust your course. You can shift your priorities. You can live a life that you love and have a rich, full existence. I'm not saying it that it will be easy, I'm saying that it will be worth it.

#GetAngry

I AM ANGRY. Aren't you too? We live in a society that is designed to keep us from manifesting our potential, all in the name of greed and power. The technology exists for cars that drive 200 miles per gallon of gas or run on water or cheap batteries, but that's not profitable for the oil industry, so we can't have that. We are literally being poisoned in our food products, our kids toys and household products contain chemicals that predisposition them to obesity and adult infertility (essentially leading to depopulation), our vaccines may cause autism and cancer, our school systems provide watered down propagandized versions of history, and on and on. All in the name of greed and power. We spend trillions to wage war, and billions to arm those who will help us (or at least not criticize us), and millions to incarcerate our own citizens, all while the homeless and needy population rises. All in the name of greed and power.

Wake up. We will spend more money today on pet food and weight loss programs and premium coffee than we do on global food aid. Wake up. We are being kept 100 years behind in progress because the people in charge don't want you getting too powerful. Wake up. Our hard earned wages fund murder and pillage across the world so that corporations can own the resources they want to sell us. Wake up. We are still in slavery, only now instead of whips and chains we suffer at the hands of debt and material possessions. Wake up. As long as we allow it, there were always be kings and subjects, owners and workers, masters and servants. Take a good look at your life and tell me you are really free... that you alone have managed to find an exemption.

Most of you will ignore this. Most of you will go on watching your "reality" television and sip on your Starbucks and drink your fluoridated tap water that dumbs you down and say "Wow, this guy has gone off the deep end." But there are some of you... who know like I know... that the first step to making things better... is getting really, really mad... and deciding you care less about what people think of you... as long as they start to think. So I will ask you this one question and take my leave: WHY IS THE WORLD THE WAY IT IS?

#BeRealistic

"Be realistic."
"What will people think?"
"Nobody else is doing that."
"That's not the way the world works."

These are just some of the phrases that kill vision and shatter dreams. You were born to be powerful, creative, imaginative, complex, thoughtful, unique, motivated individuals. When a society becomes so big that it matters and you do not, there's a problem. When a mindset becomes so restrictive that it stifles personal growth, there is a problem. Well meaning people will lovingly perpetuate their culturally imposed limitations upon you, if you allow it. But you were made for more. You are not a cog in a machine; you are living soul. Be you. Take chances. Live fully. Be real, even if that makes you "unrealistic." And learn to be okay with everyone not understanding. I'm rooting for you.

#Movement

Less distraction. More action. Be careful of becoming too comfortable. Life requires growth. Growth requires change. Change requires movement. So get a move on.

#CrazyIdeas

The next time you come up with an idea and think "That's crazy, I can't do that," ask yourself "why not?" Are you saying no to your dreams because they are unachievable, or are you simply being confined by the expectations and limits of others? In my experience I've found that the bigger the risk, the bigger the potential reward. And at the very least, the craziest plans are usually the most fun.

#Reboot

You know how you have to occasionally tune up your computer to keep it running at optimum efficiency? Well, your mind works the same way. Every now and then you need to defragment your brain and delete the temporary files that are causing stagnancy and negativity. Cookies are bits of information about places you've visited that attach themselves to your system. Ridding yourself of the mental cookies allows you to let go of preconceived notions and view the world with a new, unencumbered sight. You'll feel freer and lighter, no longer bogged down by the information overload you've received since your last update. And you'll have more open space to fill yourself with new ideas, positive affirmations, optimism, future plans, light and love, and all sorts of good things. So my advice? Clear your cache and reboot your life today. It's one of the best ways to avoid a mental malfunction and prevent a system crash.

#SayNo

Sometimes you're going to have to say NO to someone else in order to say YES to yourself. While it is good to help others, if you are not careful you'll start to put what people want FROM you above what you want FOR you. Keep your focus and know your personal limits.

#Suffering

When the stresses of life get you down; when the expectations placed upon you by you fail to be met; when you find yourself at the lowest of lows; remember, no matter isolated you feel, you are not the only one. The hurt that you think is separating you from others, is the thing that is actually connecting you. The world is suffering, from pains both real and imaginary. Wars of the flesh and of the spirit. And the solution is love. The solution is you.

#THEREISLOVE

#SayIt

Sometimes I want to tell a random friend that I love them, because I see the beauty and richness of their heart, I feel the pain of the struggle they are battling, I recognize the quiet melancholy in their eyes, and more than anything -- more than my desire to possess their beauty, more than my yearning for a physical connection to them, more than my need to feel admired by and important to someone -- I want them to know that they are not alone, that they are seen, that they are significant, and that somebody cares.

Sometimes I want to tell you I love you, and sometimes it's an innocent gesture, and sometimes it means much more. But love means putting your needs first, even if it means I never say all that I truly want to.

#NightSky

I walked outside tonight.
The sky was buzzing with light.
Not skyscrapers or billboards or planes, but the
stars shone and illuminated the pitch black
backdrop. It was magnificent.

Knowing my pitiful camera phone wouldn't be
able to convey the subtle nuances of this
visually stunning scene, I stood there lingering,
captivated. Taking in sharp breaths of the brisk
evening air, it occurred to me just how much is
around us all the time that we never see. In our
quest for success and our tendency towards
business, how many marvels have we ignored?
Then I thought, not seeing isn't always a bad
thing, as long as you have something else of
equal magnitude to focus on... or someone.

Then, as I took one last glance at nature's
canvass, I smiled in anticipation of the

beautiful distraction that somewhere in this world was awaiting my loving gaze.

#Crushing

When I see her... goose bumps.
When I think of her... chills.
When I imagine us... fever.
When she notices me... I faint.

Either she's the one or
I've got a bad case of the flu.
Either way I don't mind.
I'm just enjoying the ride.
Even if it's only in my mind.

#NoFear

If I could swim
If I could fly
I would dive into the deepest abyss
I would leap from the apex of Everest

If I could write
If I could compose
I would immortalize your name in sonnets
Making it synonymous with the symphonic

If I could paint
If I could sculpt
I'd not rest 'til your image adorned the globe
I'd chisel your perfection into every stone

If I could fight
If I was strong
I would pummel any who sought to oppose
And defeat any army that dared arose

But if I was brave

If I could talk
No fear would keep me at bay
I would at last approach you and venture to say
"Hello."

#KeepLoving

Love will always be a stronger force than hate.
Love builds. Hate destroys. Love heals you and
spreads healing to others. Hate is a cancer that
sickens you far more than those you hate. Love
creates life. Hate makes life undesirable.
Promote what you love before you bash what
you hate. Keep fighting, but keep loving too!

#Beyoutiful

There is a popular phrase that says:
"I don't want you to think like me.
I just want you to think."

Well this is my version of that:
"I don't want you to be like me.
I just want you know that it's okay to be you."

#LikeYourself

Life is a lot better when you like yourself. You should try it. And the crazy part I just discovered is you don't even have to be perfect first. Turns out, nobody is. Who knew?

#SpreadLove

Spread a little love today. A kind word, a friendly hug, a generous deed -- these things go a long way. You never know what pain someone is experiencing that your actions could alleviate. You never know what challenges someone is about to encounter that your actions could prepare them for.

Go. Give. Be. Live. Love.

#Home

Thought of the day for those who, like me, never quite feel like they belong: Home is where your love is. For some it's a city, for others a specific house, but for the lucky it's people with whom everything finally makes sense.

#4D

She wore her hair pinned up
A purple cardigan sweater
Revealing a slender and elongated neck
And the silk floral blouse beneath it
Showed just the faintest preview of her clavicle
As she rewrapped the scarf around her
To ward off the chilled breeze

It was winter
But not a particularly harsh one
Snow did not adorn the ground
Puddles were not iced over
The sun still shone
But as she stood there
Next to the red brick backdrop
Of her office building
Black wool gloves on
With the thumbs cut off
And her French tip nails exposed
A trick most likely employed to aid in texting
A cold sweat overtook me

As if Jack Frost was not just nipping at
But full on severing my nose
Freezing me in my tracks
Until nervous energy pushed me on

She was far too young for me
Not in a legal sense
We were both consenting adults
But from the standpoint of common sense
A dozen years separated us
Fine, a baker's dozen
And it was those crucial years
Where one matures
By being completely immature
And learning from their mistakes
Before ultimately reaching the contentment
Of living with and for less
When dreams taper off
And give rise to reason and responsibility
When mortgages replace Mai Tais
When family vacations replace spring break

So I had my concerns

Concerns about her maturity
Concerns about my attractiveness
Concerns about the concerns of others
I had lived my life in shadows
No, as a shadow
Never standing out
Replicating the actions of those around me
And disappearing when their light was
extinguished
Not that there wasn't more to me
There was – there is
It just always seem proper
To maintain a safe distance
From this scary thing called life

Yet here I was
Face to face with her
We had been communicating for a while
But that was online
That was digital me
That was digital her
Flesh and blood were different
Face to face was real

She saw me
And whispered something to her friend
Or co-worker
Or whoever she was
All I know is she was waiting nearby
Presumably to keep her company
And to aid in an escape if deemed necessary
Her friend whispered back
They both laughed
The friend departed
First test passed apparently

We talked
I was unusually charming
Her very presence was enchanting
Her smell rapturous
Her make-up flawless
And the lines on the nape of her neck
As she laughed at my jokes –
Wait, she laughed at my jokes!
Even the corny ones
The age factor was not one

The digital divide did not exist
We were just as comfortable
And connected as we had been
On chats, texts, and calls
4D test also passed

We spoke outside
She didn't have long
It was just her lunch break
I asked if she was hungry
But she replied when I called
Saying I was in town
And wanted to meet
She became too excited to eat
I admitted the same
Though truthfully I wanted to appear
slightly slimmer
And project lightness and youthful energy
The way one does when they first rise
And was eagerly anticipating
The Banana Berry smoothie
Waiting in my car

The co-worker reemerged
Peering through the glass entrance door
With a motion of her head
We realized it was time to return to work
And our visit was done
"My friend thinks you're hot"
She said, matter-of-factly
"Oh yeah?" I answered,
"Did you call dibs?"
She smiled that sweet smile
It was even more mesmerizing in person
Than on the profile picture that first
drew me in
"Not yet" she said slyly
"We'll see after tonight"

My eyes grew wide at the implication
When I first mentioned
I was passing through for work
And only had one night in town
She said she wasn't available
Which is why we arranged
This afternoon rendezvous

I suddenly realized this was the last test
And I had passed
I returned her smile
"Meet me here" she said
"I get off at seven"
And before I could respond
She gave me a quick peck on the cheek
And disappeared through the office doors

My stomach tugged at me
But this wasn't hunger anymore
This was the start of something new.

#Bella

She had the kind of smile
That left people both
Smitten and perturbed
Unsure if such seeming perfection
Could also possess genuineness
Photo after photo after photo
The picture became clearer
And one couldn't help but desire
To see the world through her eyes
Often she had invaded my thoughts
Her words creating piercing imagery
Showing both tender themes
And brash, sometimes bloody contrasts
I imagined her to be violent lover
Devoting herself to her man
With the same reckless abandon
That guided the rest of her life
She was a walking contradiction
Purposely practical yet spirit led
She believed in magic and fairies
Allowed the goddess free reign

While splurging on purified water
And fair trade coffee
But it worked for her
Yes, often she had invaded my thoughts
But it wasn't until I heard her voice
That she took up residence
In my dreams

#Always

It is always interesting to see
The way the tides of time
Wash away that chemical response
We once thought of as love

It is always hard to bear
The pain of sudden loss
When that which we once beheld
As permanence proves fleeting

It is always strange to learn
The resiliency of the heart
Though beaten and broken
Still somehow it ticks

It is always nice to know
That life imitates art
And the end of one chapter
Presents the start of another

It is always uplifting to read

The stories behind the smiles
Of wounds turned scars
Fading as they heal
Waiting for the real
Trading like for love
Infatuation for completion
When we learn love
Has little to do with
How we are made to feel
And all to do with
What we choose to become

#ThereIsLife

#YouMadeIt

What's the name of the monster in your past? For some of us it was depression, loneliness, suicidal thoughts, bad relationships, lousy jobs, money problems, health issues, family expectations, religious intolerance, socioeconomic standing, education, drug or alcohol addiction, mental disorders, your hometown, whatever you want to call it. We've all faced something that we were unsure if we could overcome. This is for the survivors. You made it, against all odds. Now you know that when the going gets tough, you can summon your strength and become even tougher. And knowing is half the battle.

#YourStory

Your life is a story.
It will have twists and turns.
It will have conflicts and resolutions.
Characters will come and go.
The setting may change,
The tone may lighten or darken.
Things may seem rough now,
But it's not the end of your story.
Get ready to turn the page
And start a new chapter.

#Fear

I don't know about you, but for me 99% of my inaction is due to fear. Fear of failure (experiencing the crushing blow of defeat) AND fear of success (and the anxious expectation to maintain a standard of achievement). This leads me to the "safer" option of just not trying at all. But as I've said before, falling down doesn't make one a failure, it's refusing to get back up that does. Life is a gamble, filled with ups and downs and triumphs and losses. But life is a beautiful thing, and it is meant to be lived to the fullest. Hiding from life -- hiding from yourself -- is not the safe decision, it's an empty choice that leads to regret. It's like they say in the lottery commercials "You've got to be in it to win it."

#StandOut

Don't be afraid to stand out. That person that you are: the one that struggled for acceptance, the one that always felt out of place, the one that saw the world in a different way... that person is amazing. And that person is not alone. Here's the secret they don't tell you when you're growing up -- We've all felt that way. As much as a desire to connect is a common human experience, so are thoughts of isolation. If nobody else tells you today, I'm here to tell you that you matter, you are special, and we are one.

#Maturity

One of the hardest things I've ever had to do was to take years of frustration, anger, disappointment, loneliness and jealousy, roll it into a ball, expel it from my heart, and say the following words to someone: "I'm glad you're happy."

#TheCure

I've found the best cure for listlessness is purpose, the best cure for restlessness is exploration, the best cure for longing is passion, the best cure for selfishness is necessity, the best cure for weakness is determination, the best cure for life is time, and the best cure for us is love.

#OpenYourEyes

We've all felt this way. Another day. Same old life. Nothing ever changes. But we are alive, so we are ever changing. The world around us is alive, so it is ever changing. And whether it is the innocent smile of a child you encounter, or driving to work and catching all the green lights, or even reading these words and becoming a little more aware, good things are happening all around you all the time. True, it may take a lot to change the world, but it only takes a decision to change your outlook on it.

#LetItGo

When you learn to forgive the mistakes of the
past, both made by you and by others, both
intentional and accidental, both devastating
and inconsequential, then that sometimes
miserable joyride that we call life begins to be a
lot less bitter and a lot sweeter. I don't know
about you, but I'd rather be living blissfully
than just getting by.

#Failure

So, let's get a little personal. I've been feeling a bit down about certain areas in my life that are lacking, and got to the point where I called myself a failure. But a failure is not someone who falls; it's someone who refuses to rise again. And as it is said, "If you haven't failed, you haven't lived." It's nice to know I'm in good company.

#*Masterpiece*

The things that you thought were going to break you are really the things that helped to build you. And the people that caused you the most devastating damage are really the ones that did you the biggest favor. These things found you as a block of stone, and sculpted you into a masterpiece. These people wounded you to the core, and in doing so taught you how strong and resilient you could be. Don't hate them, and don't make others pay for what they did to you. They played their part, and now you can live out yours. So forgive. Forget. And forge onward.

#LifeHappens

We've all been there. Walking along, singing a song, thinking what could possibly go wrong. And then it does. On comes a breakup, or car trouble, a bad grade, unexpected bill, random lawsuit, illness in the family. It never fails. But as much reason as we all have to crawl under the nearest rock and hide away, life will go on, with or without us. So the question we have to answer is: am I going to live my life or let life happen to me? Because we can't always choose what circumstances come, but we can choose how we respond. It's like the quote goes, "A knight in shining armor is a man who has never had his metal truly tested."

So I'm thankful for the challenges yet to come, and the battles yet to be won. For it is in these trials that we find what we are truly made of. It's in the good times that our character is shown, and it is the hard times that our character is proven.

#Mistakes

You know what? I'm thankful for my mistakes. They are plentiful. They are elaborate. They have brought me lots of grief. And they have brought me to where I am now. Everybody makes mistakes, this is true. Not everyone drops out of school out of frustration and spends ten years unsuccessfully trying to go back. Not everyone has not one, but 2 serious relationships with women that said they wanted to spend their life with you end within 6 months of each other, only to have both of these women married to other people six months later. Not everyone takes a job they hate to provide for a family they love, do a great job, and still gets fired and falsely accused of embezzlement. And not everybody can sit here and laugh about it after getting through it all. Yeah, this has been the crazy journey I've been on. And you know what? It's all good.

One thing I've learned about life is that it goes on, with or without you. And the things that really matter are not the material possessions or the desire to get back at people or even the heartache suffered along the way. The things that matter are the people who bring joy into your life, and the passions that you were always afraid to explore, and the hearts that you can touch along the way. My mistakes have made me an encourager, because they've made me need encouraging. They've made me focused on my goals, back in school and a published author, all because I never want to be expected to compromise my morals for a paycheck again. They've led me to connect with hundreds of people, to always be available when someone reaches out for advice or compassion. And I kind of like who I am now, which is something I hadn't been able to say for a long time. So you know what? I am thankful to be able to say: my name is Jelani, and I'm a screw-up. And I am proud of it.

#Holidays

Have you ever noticed how the holiday season gets you to thinking about family and friends you haven't seen in a long time? And you begin to wonder what exactly it was that made you lose touch.

Those close friends that suddenly vanished. People whose weddings you were in that are like strangers now. Exes and BFFs and relatives and coworkers; people that occupied a big space in your life for a time, and now don't. Why is that? I'm sure there are a lot of reasons, but one consistent theme I've been hearing in my travels is guilt.

People feel guilty about something they did to a friend, or failed to do for a friend, or for a personal shortcoming that they were ashamed for a friend to find out.

Everyone's situation is different, and I'm not making light of anyone's feelings, but if you want to grow into the more in you, it's time to let it go.

Forgive Them.
Forgive Yourself.

Not every connection is meant to last a lifetime, but if you are still thinking about them or worried about what they think about you, then guess what? You are still connected. Now is the time of renewal and closure. Only you know which one you need. But it starts with forgiveness, and an end to the guilt and shame you've carried far too long.

Be Free.

#ExerciseYourFaith

I've come to realize something. We all have our insecurities. We all have those areas of our lives that we are sensitive about. We shy away from situations that bring these things to light and fly to others that we have confident in. We think that by focusing on our strengths we can avoid our weaknesses being discovered.

For example, I used to love to sing but because I was around other people with what I thought was more talent, I was deathly afraid to perform. I spent years writing melodies and developing my voice, but all I have to show for it is a notebook of 200+ songs that no one has ever heard. In fact, I was so terrified to bare that part of me that I actually started a brief rap career so that I could still be in music without taking too big a risk.

Then one morning I was in the gym and it hit me. Our fears and insecurities are like unworked muscles. Have you seen those bodybuilders with huge chests and arms... and itty bitty legs? That's how we live our lives. And it's not because we can't work legs, it's because we have a mental or emotional block that pushes to keep working upper body because that's what we know or have been accepted for.

I'm here to tell you today that all of you is glorious. You have the potential be awesome, and not just in those things you are known for, even in those secret parts of you that you have yet to reveal. It's time to train yourself; build your body of accomplishments; exercise your faith and take a chance.

#Grief

It's sad to hear so many stories about heartache and death recently. My heart goes out to those suffering through a great loss. Often times, there are no right words to share with those in pain; what's most important is to just be there.

But this is a message for the living, for the survivors. For those willing to adopt a perspective of appreciation. For those willing to not let the frailty of life keep them from living to the fullest, from trying again, and from experiencing others along the way. Put your love glasses on.

#Memories

I love to reminisce. Flipping through photo albums packed with memories of times gone by seems to settle me. For some reason even the harshest of memories are mellowed by the rose colored hue of hindsight. Even listening to what was your favorite album 5 or 6 years ago can transport you back to that time and place, bringing with it the joy of that time. A familiar fragrance can send you back to your first love. The taste of a delicacy you had on a vacation can flood you with vivid images. But the thing is, that in order to be able to enjoy your life's experiences, you have to first create them. So the thing I love most about reminiscing is that it reminds me how far I've come, how much I've done, and how limitless my future can be.

#Movement

There's a flip side to reminiscing. When all you
do is live in the past, dwelling in the mistakes
of time gone by or rejoicing in your former
triumphs as if it will never get better for you, it
makes it real hard to have any tangible
existence in the present. Life requires
movement. Don't give up and reside in that old
place. If it was great, guess what? You have the
capacity for better. If it was miserable, that
doesn't mean you will repeat the past. Too
many people are playing it safe because
they've been hurt and now they think it's better
to not want any more than they have and be
disappointed when their desires fail to
manifest. I know, I've been there, hiding from
life. But you create what you emit. "As a man
thinketh in his heart, so is he." Dwell in the
past and the past is all you'll have. I say shoot
for the moon; even if you miss you'll still land
among the stars.

#TheBestPart

You know the best part of life? All of it. The easy, the hard, the challenging and heart-breaking, the vivid and breathtaking, the amazing and the ordinary, the frenetic and the predictable, the hurt, the glorious, the ecstatic, the savory, the succulent, the disgusting, the gut-wrenching, the miraculous, the awkward. It's all good. It's all a gift. Embrace it. Love it. Live it.

#Bloopers

You know something? We've all done really, really stupid things at one point or another in our life. Like that relationship that everyone said was doomed, but we knew better... until things fell apart. Or that awkward moment when you felt so comfortable with some friends that you showed a little too much of your weird side... and got odd, silent stares. Maybe you tripped in public and landed in a puddle or forgot to put your phone on silent and got a phone call in the middle of a funeral or looked a pretty girl walking down the street and crashed into the car in front of you... or maybe these are just things that happened to me.

The point is, these things that we do are horrible in the moment, painful for a while, embarrassing for a long time, but eventually just become funny. It doesn't kill you, it gives you character, and a lot of memories to enjoy.

So if you will, take a second to think back on your personal blooper reel and have a good laugh at yourself.

#Forgiveness

Have you ever asked someone for forgiveness and gotten it, but then couldn't get over it yourself? Whether it's from committing a mistake or simply from awakening to new truths, personal condemnation is a fruitless endeavor that results in stagnancy. That voice in your head that tries to keep you down with guilt and shame is a LIAR. Forgive yourself and be new... and be more.

#Correction

I used to get upset when people corrected me. I don't mean something like, "Oh you misspelled that word," I mean when someone questions your life decisions. Often we find ourselves defined by the company we keep. We get caught up in our little groups and titles and jobs and traditions, and if anyone steps out of line with an original thought they are considered "off." It *used* to bother me.

I so wanted to do the right thing, be accepted, get that pat on the back and an "Atta boy!" So when correction was presented I shut down, I hid, I argued, I felt worthless, I lost confidence in my decisions. Then I came to understand something, there is a difference between correction and opinion.

Correction is a legitimate, thought provoking, soul reminding tough love offering that comes from a place of wanting the best for someone.

To offer me correction you must first: 1) know me on more than a surface level, and 2) have an idea of where I want my life to go. I'll gladly take that and make adjustments if I'm off track. However, if you don't know these things, and you are merely confounded because I'm not doing what you would do or want me to do, and as a result are telling me that I am wrong for making choices that don't fit with your perception of me... that is an opinion.

Understanding the difference between the two has helped me immensely to rid myself of unnecessary guilt, shame, and doubt that was imposed on me by the expectations of others. I don't run anymore. I don't hide anymore. And since I realize that not everyone has received such freedom, I just let them talk and nod and smile. And then I go on and live my life.

#WatchMe

You know generally when someone questions your ability or right to do something it's because they don't feel that they have the right or ability to do that thing. So the next time someone asks you "Who said you could do that?" turn around and ask them "Who said you couldn't?"

#Emotional

I'm the type of person that would rather experience physical pain than emotional pain. If you punch me, it may hurt for a moment, but I'll recover and move on. But nothing wounds deeper and causes more sleepless nights than the crippling emotional pain of loss, heartache, loneliness, or misunderstandings.

#*Listen*

LISTEN!!!

No, not to me.

Listen to your heart.
Trust the voice within you.
The one that rings the truest.
And follow your intuition.
The first time.
In the moment.
Without hesitation.

Again, not because I said to.
Do it because you already feel it.
Do it because you already know.
Do it and let yourself connect with the eternal.

#TheSoundOfSilence

There is a silence
That few know exists
In which there is no emptiness
No lack of sound or life
Rather in this soulful quiet
Lies the absence of distraction

Banished is the noise that blinds
Replaced with an overwhelming
All encompassing
Completely consuming
Awe inspiring
Destructive peace
That returns the Mind
Body and Soul
To a state of oneness
So that what is not known
Can be felt
And what is not felt
Can be lived
And what is not lived

Is still somehow known

Deep within this silence
The You-niverse is revealed
Nay, remembered
As the deafening tone
Of a steady heartbeat
Tunes its cadence
To the eternal rhythm of life.

#IsleofHope

From whence has this day come?
The genteel breeze politely
Caressing the weathered leaves
Of the Majestic Oak
Centuries of wisdom concealed
Within the sturdy confines
Of its rough and noble trunk
Sunlight streaming through the coils
Of Spanish Moss dangling
From its haphazardly protruding limbs
Creating a kaleidoscopic display
More engaging than the most
Technically advance laser show
The ground is soft and malleable
Moist yet not wet
Only leaving the faintest trace
Of moisture and an earthy scent
On those who take delight
In laying prostrate upon it

The assumption is that nature

Has nothing to offer
Has no comfort to provide
Has no mystery to unlock
But out in this place
This Isle of Hope
With the tepid air brimming
With the cries of a multitude
Of species existing in a harmonic
Explosion of life
Away from the familiar constant
Buzzing and chirping and beeping
That interrupts life's rhythm
And in the presence of the original
Buzzing and chirping and beeping
In synchronicity with life's rhythm
I have found
More than plant
More than animal
I have found
My humanity

#Rebirth

There is a place
Between night and morning
Between joy and mourning
Between darkness and light
Between descent and flight
This is the place where life is found
This is the place where love is born
This is the climax
After the rising action
Before the denouement
This is anticipation
This is the moment of creation
Word becoming deed becoming reality
This is the sweet spot
And this is where I reside
Waiting
Plotting
Chomping at the bit
Completely engaged
Consistently enraptured
Ever present

Pregnant with purpose
Ready to experience
Rebirth ◉

#IcarusFlew

Icarus flew too close to the sun
That was his downfall
But should his demise
Be blamed on him for believing
He could soar with impunity
Or his father Daedalus
For first crafting the wings
And showing Icarus
It was possible to fly

Daedalus flew low
He took the safe approach
But Icarus found such delight
In the majesty of flight
He joyously flapped for new heights

This sparks the question
Is it better to know your limits
And remain at conservative levels
Or is it better to believe
You are truly limitless

And enjoy every moment's thrill
Even if in the end
When the heat rises
You suffer a fall

Icarus flew too close to the sun
But the part too many forget
Is that *Icarus flew.*

#DontSettle

Aren't you tired of settling?
Just okay is not good enough anymore.
I'm not content with getting by.
I need more.
I want it all.

I want to embrace my future.
I want to give life a big, wet, sloppy kiss.
I want to fly without fear.
I want passionate partnerships.
I want electric experiences.
I want to give myself over to the current.
I want to flow with pulse of the universe.
These rules no longer apply.
Your boxes can't contain me.

I am spirit.
I am stardust.
I am Adam's atoms.
Before the fall.

In alignment.

As it was.
As it is.
As it will be.
No guilt.
No shame.
Feverish freedom.
Sans separation.
Eternal essence.

I want it back.
Don't you?

#MindsEye

I've been experiencing
The strangest sensations
My mind in a fog
My heart so conflicted
My energy screaming
But without direction

They say it's your vibration
They say focus your chi
They say submit to the Father
They say so many things

What is right or wrong?
Who is right or wrong?
Is there right or wrong?

I pondered the Euthyphro Dilemma
For years before I knew it existed
And now that I have become aware
My mind is even more inexorably twisted

This is not a poem
This is just a thought
One of millions
Racing and colliding in my cerebrum

I am not a man
I am just a soul
On a journey of comprehension
Before shifting to another dimension

Experiencing an internal transfiguration
That confounds those who thought they knew me
Including myself

Where do I go from here
When the elevation of my concentration
Battles daily inundation from fluoridation
When I attempt meditation
And instead find inspiration
When I see opportunities for cooperation
But am thwarted by the societal expectation
To remain in isolation

And love, yes even love –
That oft-confused chemical response
That is so much more than the little we experience
On cool Autumn nights snuggled within blankets
Lips chapped from our beloved's kisses
Or on empty days when we are reminded
That there is someone thinking about us
Via a smiley face text from another empty person
Seeking to be validated in return
Two souls desperate to matter
Not realizing that are the very essence of the universe
Artfully composed into flesh vessels –
Has lost its luster
Because we expect to feel it all of the time
But love, like us, is nothing short than Divine
You don't feel it, you are it

There is such beauty
That no one ever sees
Because they don't look
Past the forest for the trees
We have such greatness
That never seems to come

Because we don't realize
We are all one

Am I the only one aware?
Am I the only one who cares?

My mind is like a bottle of soda
Shaken, disturbed, ready to pop
Eruption is imminent
But what will come out is unknown

I am not a poet
I am just a seeker
Trying to find the path home.

#ThereIsTime

#ILoveMe

I love me.

Does that sound vain? Do you think I care? It has taken me my entire 34 years of life to be able to honestly say those three words. I've always felt different, like an outsider who would never fit in.

In my hometown I get strange looks from people that treat me like there's something wrong with me because I'm not content with... less.

To friends I'm the creative guy who seems to be able to do anything (when in reality I'm just good at faking), and that turned me into the one you call when you need something done. And all I wanted to be was the one they called when they didn't need a thing, but just wanted to be around me.

In relationships I took that insecurity and made myself fit into whatever role the other person needed. I became so skilled at pretending that I forgot who I was. I wanted people to love me so much that I became someone I hated.

And then I lost everything.

I began to find myself again, but now I was so consumed with the past, the loss, the mistakes that I began to hate myself even more. But then the realization came. Someone shared with me 2 things their therapist told them.

1. You are a FHB - Fallible Human Being. That means you will make mistakes. And
2. You are already worthy.

You don't have to be perfect. Nobody is. You don't have to be defined by your past. Every moment you live is another opportunity to make a positive choice... to create a better future. It's been a long road.

I've lived several realities: son, brother, husband, father, writer, rapper, minister, employee, boss, business owner, poet, activist, friend, divorcee, fat guy, less fat guy, singer, actor, Facebook encourager in chief, boyfriend, empath, dog owner, student, and so much more.

But liking any of those roles didn't not translate into liking the guy that was playing them. I had to learn to love me: the scatterbrained, hopeless romantic, vegetable juicing, documentary watching, songwriting, Broadway musical loving, non-dancing, sometimes cool/sometimes dorky, long winded writing guy that I am.

And when I got to the point where I didn't change my behavior or demeanor to adapt to people around me, I realized I didn't care what

they thought of me, because I am secure in
what I think of me. And I so very thankful that
I can finally say: I LOVE ME.

#OwnIt

"Whatever you do, own it."

I heard my sister speak these words to her then six-year-old son and it instantly struck me. Not just because of its profundity, but also the layered interpretations of the message. As I stood there marveled thinking I understood, she explained her meaning to his waiting gaze. I pause for a second so that you can think about this statement, and see which of our two understandings you were immediately drawn to.

"Whatever you do, own it."

Her meaning – The system is rigged. Society favors those in charge. So while some struggle in anonymity for change, equality, and fairness, you should go into life with a clear understanding of the world you're entering. So if you goal is to be a football player, learn the game with an intent on being a team owner. If your interests lie in culinary designs, don't settle for a spot as a Sous Chef, have your own show on the food network with a chain of 5-star restaurants. Don't just punch a time clock at an office; put your name on the building. Whatever you do, own it.

I heard her detail these wise words of advice and was floored. If only, I thought, someone would've inspired me to reach beyond the confines of the box life told me existed before I had been swallowed up in student loans, an unfocused job history, and poor credit and relationship decisions.

Like many my age, I still find myself climbing out of ever-deepening hole entirely of my own making, with just my grit, spit, and determination to rescue me from the abyss. And while we re-teach ourselves positive life choices, I saw her look to the future and prepare a boy to become a man…a king amongst giants.

"Whatever you do, own it."

My meaning – One of the big phrases you hear these days is personal responsibility. It is today's counter-argument to an interventionist society. For example, people say we can't invest in education; parents just need to take personal responsibility for their kids (okay that's a hornet's nest I didn't intend to touch). Anyway, when I heard the "own it" principle, I immediately went to personal responsibility. In a roundabout way, I took it as a "do the crime, do the time" interpolation, but not just in a negative connotation. If you get that girl pregnant, own it. If you graduate magna cum laude, own it. "Own it" to me was a way garnishing confidence in one's self and showing the world that they don't have any say in who I say I am.

Talk show host Montel Williams has a motivational speech that I like entitled "Who Owns the Definition of You." In it, Montel talks about the labels that people will put on us our entire life and that ultimately it is up to each of us to decide to accept or reject these labels. You have to "own" who you are; a move that brings with it a confidence and swagger liken to the famous George Jefferson strut from the television show "The Jeffersons." I heard my sister tell her son, inadvertently mind you, to free himself from the perceptions of others, search within for his true self, and walk head up and chest high sure of himself from that day forward.

"Whatever you do, own it."

#NewDay

Let today's shortcomings go. Failing does not make you a failure, it makes you experienced. Every new day is a new opportunity to do more, to live more, to be more. Embrace your newness, embrace your more. I'll be rooting for you.

#MyGoal

My goal today: spread love.
My goal tomorrow: spread love.
My goal forever: I think you get it.

#YouHaveTime

Here's a thought: Phones work both ways.
That person can call you just as easily as you
can them. They don't know what you've been
through. Phones work both ways. You can stop
feeling so entitled and call that person you're
waiting on. You don't know what they've been
through. Sometimes that call won't come or be
made. And that's okay. You can't make
someone love you... or want you... or even
tolerate you. You can't make yourself feel or
want what is not there. Don't settle for good
enough for now. You deserve amazing. Not
only that... you are amazing.

Life is about choices, and often those choices
are made from a mindset of urgency. But here's
the thing, you have time. Time to figure it out.
Time to become. Time to develop relationships.
Time to try and fail and try again. And even
though you have time, you might not need it.
Sometimes you just know. Sometimes it

happens in an instant. Trust yourself; you know more than you think you do.

More often than not, it is fear that holds us back from making those truly outrageous decisions. We know that they could change our lives forever, but we won't know if it's for the better or worse until we try. It boils down to a matter of faith. Either way you are choosing to believe in something, either that you'll succeed (or gain experience trying) or fail (or be safe by not trying). So, what do you believe?

We all get the same 24 hours every day. What you do with them is up to you. Regardless if you're working or studying or caring for families during most of your day, I implore you not to squander the precious little time you have left trapped in fear, doubt, and worry.

I've said it before and I'll say it again: there are so many things in this world fighting for your attention and your heart, so many causes for you to devote yourself to, so many ideologies for you to ascribe to; but if you are going to wholeheartedly believe in anything, I hope you start with you.

#GetYou

Here's a free tip: Those who are supposed to "get" you already do. Those who don't, can catch up or get left behind. Don't waste your life trying to fit in where you clearly don't when there is a place where you will just waiting for your arrival.

I'm not telling you what I think, I'm telling you what I know... I'm telling you what I've lived.

#JustBe

Hey.

Do me a favor.

Just for a minute.

Forget about that thing.

You know, that problem on your mind.

The reason you can't sleep or concentrate.

Why you have anxiety issues and nervousness.

Not always, but just enough to realize
something's off.

Are you done denying it and ready to
acknowledge what I'm saying?

Good. Now forget it. Breathe. Relax. Clear your
mind. Find your center. Imagine something
truly beautiful. A sunrise. A child's smile. A
precious memory. The kiss of your beloved.
Live in that image. And for the next sixty
seconds... just be.

Feel better? That was to remind you that your
mind possesses a powerful force. The more

you focus on something, the more it manifests itself in you. That's not to say if you think about a million dollars you'll win the lottery, but you might start to feel more wealthy and carry yourself with an air of success. And if you imagine yourself flying you probably won't get super powers, but you may feel lighter both physically and emotionally. Conversely, the more you dwell on that problem in your life (instead of its solution), the more likely you are to create negative emotions and physical symptoms in you. You can literally become worried sick. So the next time that thing (and we all have one) begins to wreak havoc on your day, remember that you have the power to change your thoughts, and with it your reality.

#TheJourney

The highway speaks to me
There are volumes in its silence
Crafting a call to all comers
Like a melody waiting for notation
Like a poem yet to be written
Like a truth existing for eons
Desiring to be discovered
But only revealed to those who seek
Miles to go and missions to complete.

#*Time*

If it's your bedtime, then sleep. If it's morning where you are, then arise. But no matter where you are, and no matter what time it is, and no matter what challenges the day may hold, I beseech you, live.

#Still

Heart still beating.
Lungs still breathing.
I'm still hoping.
I'm still reaching.

Eyes still seeing.
Mind still thinking.
I'm still loving.
I'm still living.

#ThereIsMe

#ThereIsMe

Those who truly know me know that I am a walking contradiction, and that I am just fine with that. They know that I am very serious about the world, but don't take myself too seriously. That I can be fiercely sarcastic, but would never intentionally hurt anyone's feelings. That I pride myself on being strong and levelheaded in difficult situations, but at the same time I am a very sensitive soul that holds onto emotional hurt. They know that if you contact me asking for advice or encouragement I will drop what I am doing to help, but will rarely ever ask for assistance for myself, even when desperately needed. That I am friendly and extroverted online, but am shy and introverted in person. That one of my passions is to see people live their dreams, but found my own goals stagnant for years out of fear of failure and meeting the expectations of others. That I fervently believe that every person has the potential and ability to live an awesome life, while being the first to tell you "I'm not that special." That my real talent is not writing or speaking or music or marketing or any of the endless things I do; my real talent lies in seeing things and instantly knowing how to make them better. They know that this talent mixed with my heart to see others succeed has led me to agree to help people with their business ideas, and ended some friendships when I felt it was time to move on while they wanted me to keep building their vision at the expense of my own. They know that my life, while seemingly filled with "friends" and "family" is actually a very lonely one, and I have struggled with depression and self-esteem issues for years. They know that I usually play things safe, not out of a fear of adventure, but rather out of a fear of not being around for my kids or completing my life's great work. They know that my entire life I have been looking for love, and that for the same amount of time I have worried about it coming just to disappear again. They know that there is an unexplored depth within me, and if the day ever comes that I truly give in to it, I am liable to change the world. And those who truly know me are aware, just like I am, that I am right on the precipice of becoming who and what I was always meant to be. This is why I own my truth. This is why I bare my soul. For when that time arrives I want someone to look at me and say "He's just like me. The same perfectly imperfect work of art. And if he can do it, then so can I." Yes, I believe you -- WE -- can.

These are the facts: I am not your savior. I am not your hero. I can't heal your broken heart. I cannot make you go on. I absolutely cannot solve your problems nor fix the world alone. What I am is your brother, your friend, an ally, an admirer, a co-conspirator, a commiserator, an encourager, a shoulder to cry and/or lean on. What I can do is love you until you love yourself, share my path and my journey in the hopes that you either relate and feel less alone or are inspired to realign your life's direction, and root for you the whole way. I will never tell you what to do; I believe we all need to make our own choices and live with our own consequences. I can celebrate with you in your triumphs, doubling your joy. I can comfort you in your tragedies, halving your pain. And it would be my great pleasure and privilege to stand with you as we repair this damaged world of ours. What I am is human and all I can be is me. Won't you please join me? This book's ending is our journey's beginning. Are you ready?

#BeAwesome
#OwnYourTruth
#Believe
#BeLove
#YouGotThis

#ThereIsMore

J.M. Weldon is a writer, humorist, motivational speaker, award winning poet, and self-proclaimed "hopeful romantic." His professional background includes stints as a radio host, Christian music artist, and celebrity ghost writer.

He is the author of four books, including the poetic journey *Intertwined* and scathing comedy *You're Not That Special*. He is also the proud father of two wonderful children. He currently resides in Savannah, Georgia. You can learn more about the author, as well as view his current and upcoming works at www.jmweldon.com.

www.ingramcontent.com/pod-product-compliance
Lightning Source LLC
Chambersburg PA
CBHW032033040426
42449CB00007B/873